F L U T E
ONE HUNDRED
C L A S S I C A L
T H E M E S

Exclusive Distributors:
Music Sales Limited
8/9 Frith Street, London W1V 5TZ, England.
Music Sales Corporation
225 Park Avenue South, New York, NY10003, USA.
Music Sales Pty Limited
120 Rothschild Avenue, Rosebery, NSW 2018, Australia.

This book © Copyright 1991 by Wise Publications
Order No. AM84179
ISBN 0-7119-2589-5

Design by Hutton Staniford
Front cover photography by Stuart MacGregor

Music Sales' complete catalogue lists thousands of titles
and is free from your local music shop, or direct from
Music Sales Limited.
Please send a cheque/postal order for £1.50 for postage to:
Music Sales Limited, Newmarket Road, Bury St. Edmunds,
Suffolk IP33 3YB.

Your Guarantee of Quality
As publishers, we strive to produce every book to the
highest commercial standards.
The music has been freshly engraved and the book has
been carefully designed to minimise awkward page turns
and to make playing from it a real pleasure.
Particular care has been given to specifying acid-free,
neutral-sized paper which has not been chlorine bleached
but produced with special regard for the environment.
Throughout, the printing and binding have been planned
to ensure a sturdy, attractive publication which should
give years of enjoyment.
If your copy fails to meet our high standards, please inform
us and we will gladly replace it.

Printed in the United Kingdom by
Caligraving Limited, Thetford, Norfolk.

Wise Publications
London/New York/Sydney

A Musical Joke
(K.522, 4th movement) Mozart 4
A Policeman's Lot Is Not A Happy One
('The Pirates of Penzance') Sullivan 4
Air On The G String
(Suite No.3, 2nd movement) Bach 5
Autumn
(The Four Seasons, No.3, 1st movement) Vivaldi 6
Autumn
(The Four Seasons, No.3, 3rd movement) Vivaldi 6
Barcarolle
('The Tales of Hoffmann') Offenbach 7
Berceuse
(Dolly Suite Op.56) Fauré 8
Bolero
Ravel 8
Bridal March
('Lohengrin') Wagner 9
Brigg Fair
(An English Rhapsody) Delius 10
Brindisi
('La Traviata') Verdi 10
Che Farò Senza Euridice
('Orfeo ed Euridice') Gluck 11
Clarinet Concerto
(K.622, 2nd movement) Mozart 11
Clair de Lune
(Suite Bergamasque) Debussy 12
Eine Kleine Nachtmusik
(K.525, 1st movement) Mozart 12
Emperor Waltz
(Op.437) Strauss 13
España
(Rhapsody for Orchestra) Chabrier 14
Farandole
(L'Arlésienne Suite No.2) Bizet 14
For He Is An Englishman
('HMS Pinafore') Sullivan 15
Für Elise
Beethoven 15
Galop Infernal
('Orpheus in the Underworld') Offenbach 16
Gaudeamus Igitur
(Academic Festival Overture Op.80) Brahms 16
Gavotte
(Suite No.3, 3rd movement) Bach 17
Golliwogg's Cake Walk
(Children's Corner) Debussy 18
Gymnopédie No.1
Satie 18
Habanera
('Carmen') Bizet 19

He Shall Feed His Flock
('Messiah') Handel 20
Horn Concerto No.4
(K.495, 3rd movement) Mozart 20
Hornpipe
(The Water Music) Handel 21
Humoresque
(Op.101 No.7) Dvořák 21
Hungarian Dance No.5
Brahms 22
Jerusalem
Parry 22
Jupiter – I Vow To Thee, My Country
(The Planets Suite) Holst 23
La Calinda
('Koanga') Delius 24
Là Ci Darem La Mano
('Don Giovanni') Mozart 24
La Donna È Mobile
('Rigoletto') Verdi 25
Land of Hope and Glory
(Pomp & Circumstance March No.1 Op.39) Elgar 26
Largo – Ombra Mai Fù
('Xerxes') Handel 27
Les Sylphides
(Prelude Op.28 No.7) Chopin 27
March
(The Nutcracker Suite Op.71) Tchaikovsky 28
Minuet II
(Music For The Royal Fireworks) Handel 28
Morning
(Peer Gynt Suite No.1 Op.46) Grieg 29
Nimrod
(Enigma Variations Op.36) Elgar 30
Nocturne
('A Midsummer Night's Dream' Op.61) Mendelssohn 30
Non Più Andrai
('The Marriage of Figaro') Mozart 31
O For The Wings Of A Dove
('Hear My Prayer') Mendelssohn 32
Ode To Joy
(Symphony No.9 Op.125, 4th movement) Beethoven 33
One Fine Day
('Madame Butterfly') Puccini 33
Pavane
(Op.50) Fauré 34
Piano Concerto
(Op.16, 1st movement) Grieg 34
Piano Concerto – 'Elvira Madigan'
(K.467, 2nd movement) Mozart 35
Piano Concerto No.1
(Op.23, 1st movement) Tchaikovsky 35

Piano Concerto No.3
(*Op.37, 1st movement*) *Beethoven* 36
Piano Concerto No.5 – 'The Emperor'
(*Op.73 2nd movement*) *Beethoven* 36
Polovtsian Dances
(*'Prince Igor'*) *Borodin* 37
Pie Jesu
(*Requiem Op.48*) *Fauré* 38
Pomp & Circumstance March No.4
(*Op.39*) *Elgar* 38
Poor Wand'ring One
(*'The Pirates Of Penzance'*) *Sullivan* 39
Prelude
(*L'Arlésienne Suite No.1*) *Bizet* 40
Prelude to Act III
(*Lohengrin*) *Wagner* 40
Promenade
(*Pictures At An Exhibition*) *Mussorgsky* 41
Prince Igor Overture
Borodin 42
Radetzky March
(*Op.228*) *Strauss* 42
Romeo and Juliet
(*Fantasy Overture*) *Tchaikovsky* 43
Rondeau
(*'Abdelazar'*) *Purcell* 44
Rosamunde
(*Entr'acte Act III*) *Schubert* 44
Salut d'Amour
(*Op.12*) *Elgar* 45
Serenade
Schubert 45
Spartacus – 'The Onedin Line'
Khatchaturian 46
Spring
(*The Four Seasons, No.1, 1st movement*) *Vivaldi* 47
St Anthony Chorale
(*Variations on a Theme of Haydn Op.56a*) *Brahms* 47
Swan Lake
(*Op.20, Opening of Act II*) *Tchaikovsky* 48
Symphonie Fantastique
(*Op.14, 4th movement*) *Berlioz* 48
Symphony No.1
(*Op.68, 4th movement*) *Brahms* 49
Symphony No.3
(*Op.90, 3rd movement*) *Brahms* 49
Symphony No.3 – 'The Eroica'
(*Op.55, 2nd movement*) *Beethoven* 50
Symphony No.5
(*Op.64, 2nd movement*) *Tchaikovsky* 50
Symphony No.6 – 'The Pastoral'
(*Op.68, 5th movement*) *Beethoven* 51

Symphony No.6 – 'The Pathétique'
(*Op.74, 1st movement*) *Tchaikovsky* 51
Symphony No.9 – 'The Great'
(*2nd movement*) *Schubert* 52
Symphony No.9 – 'From the New World'
(*Op.95, 2nd movement*) *Dvořák* 52
Symphony No.9 – 'From the New World'
(*Op.95, 4th movement*) *Dvořák* 53
Symphony No.94 – 'The Surprise'
(*2nd movement*) *Haydn* 53
Take A Pair Of Sparkling Eyes
(*'The Gondoliers'*) *Sullivan* 54
Tannhäuser Overture
Wagner 54
The Blue Danube
(*Waltz, Op.314*) *Strauss* 55
The Merry Peasant
(*Album for the Young Op.68 No.10*) *Schumann* 56
The Trout Piano Quintet
(*4th movement*) *Schubert* 56
Toreador's Song
(*'Carmen'*) *Bizet* 57
Tristesse
(*Étude Op.10 No.3*) *Chopin* 57
Trumpet Voluntary
(*'The Prince of Denmark's March'*) *Clarke* 58
Valse
(*'Coppélia'*) *Delibes* 58
Violin Concerto
(*Op.77, 2nd movement*) *Brahms* 59
Violin Concerto
(*Op.61, 2nd movement*) *Elgar* 60
Violin Concerto
(*Op.64, 2nd movement*) *Mendelssohn* 60
Waltz
(*'The Sleeping Beauty' Op.66*) *Tchaikovsky* 61
Wedding March
(*'A Midsummer Night's Dream' Op.61*) *Mendelssohn* 62
William Tell Overture
Rossini 62
Your Tiny Hand Is Frozen
(*'La Bohème'*) *Puccini* 63
24th Caprice for Solo Violin
Paganini 64

A MUSICAL JOKE

(K.522, 4th movement) Mozart

A POLICEMAN'S LOT IS NOT A HAPPY ONE

('The Pirates of Penzance') Sullivan

AIR ON THE G STRING

(Suite No.3, 2nd movement) Bach

AUTUMN

(The Four Seasons, No.3, 1st movement) Vivaldi

AUTUMN

(The Four Seasons, No.3, 3rd movement) Vivaldi

BARCAROLLE

('The Tales Of Hoffmann') Offenbach

BERCEUSE

(Dolly Suite Op.56) Fauré

BOLERO

Ravel

BRIDAL MARCH

('Lohengrin') Wagner

Moderato con moto

cresc.   *f*   *dim.*

9

BRIGG FAIR

(An English Rhapsody) Delius

With easy movement ♩.=66
Allegretto leggiero

BRINDISI

('La Traviata') Verdi

Allegretto

CHE FARÒ SENZA EURIDICE

('Orfeo ed Euridice') Gluck

Andante con moto

CLARINET CONCERTO

(K.622, 2nd movement) Mozart

Adagio

CLAIRE DE LUNE

(Suite Bergamasque) Debussy

Andante - très expressif

tempo rubato

peu à peu cresc. et animé

dim. molto

EINE KLEINE NACHTMUSIK

(K.525, 1st movement) Mozart

Allegro

EMPEROR WALTZ

(op.437) Strauss

Tempo di valse

ben legato

ESPAÑA

(Rhapsody for Orchestra) Chabrier

FARANDOLE

(L'Arlésienne Suite No.2) Bizet

FOR HE IS AN ENGLISHMAN

('HMS Pinafore') Sullivan

FÜR ELISE

Beethoven

GALOP INFERNAL

('Orpheus in the Underworld') Offenbach

GAUDEAMUS IGITUR

(Academic Festival Overture Op.80) Brahms

GAVOTTE

(Suite No.3, 3rd movement) Bach

GOLLIWOGG'S CAKE WALK

(Children's Corner) Debussy

Allegro giusto

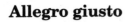

GYMNOPÉDIE NO.1

Satie

Lent et douloureux

HABAÑERA

('Carmen') Bizet

Allegretto quasi andantino

HE SHALL FEED HIS FLOCK

('The Messiah') Handel

Larghetto e piano

HORN CONCERTO NO.4

(K.495, 3rd movement) Mozart

Allegro vivace

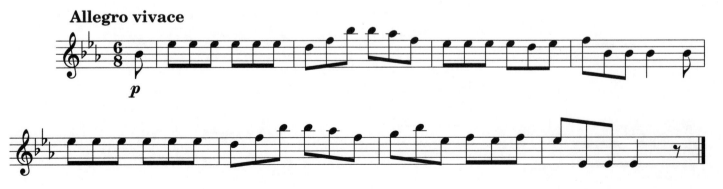

HORNPIPE

(The Water Music) Handel

Alla Hornpipe

HUMORESQUE

(Op.101 No.7) Dvořák

Poco lento e grazioso

21

HUNGARIAN DANCE NO.5

Brahms

Allegro

JERUSALEM

Parry

Slow but with animation

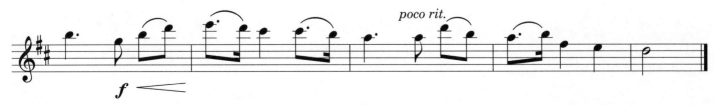

JUPITER - I VOW TO THEE MY COUNTRY

(The Planets Suite) Holst

Andante maestoso

LA CALINDA

('Koanga') Delius

LÀ CI DAREM LA MANO

('Don Giovanni') Mozart

LA DONNA È MOBILE

('Rigoletto') Verdi

LAND OF HOPE AND GLORY

(Pomp & Circumstance March No.1 Op.39) Elgar

Allegro (largamente)

LARGO – OMBRA MAI FÙ

('Xerxes') Handel

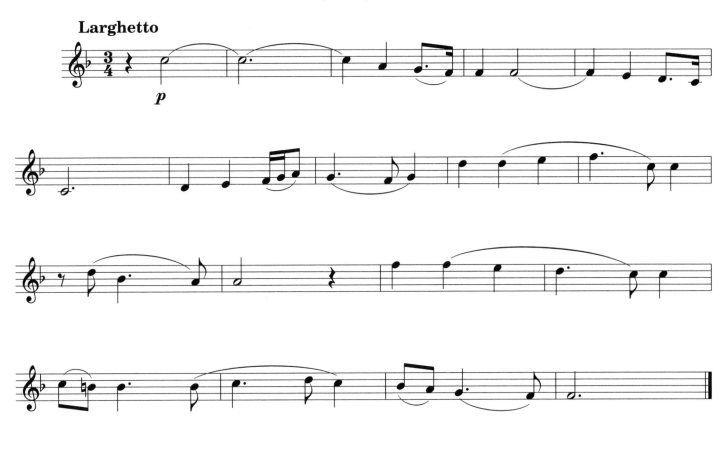

LES SYLPHIDES

(Prelude Op.28 No.7) Chopin

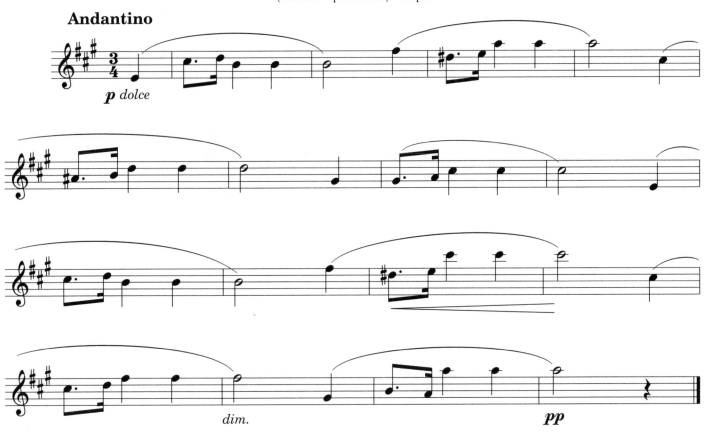

MARCH

(The Nutcracker Suite Op.71) Tchaikovsky

MINUET II

(Music for the Royal Fireworks) Handel

MORNING

(Peer Gynt Suite No.1 Op.46) Grieg

Allegretto pastorale

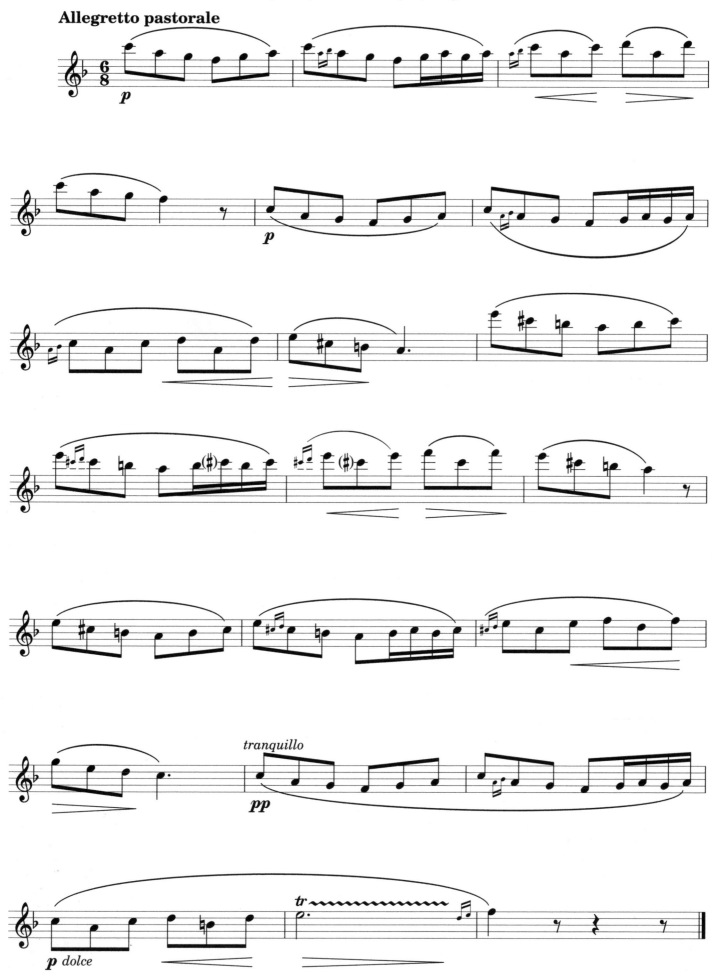

NIMROD

(Enigma Variations Op.36) Elgar

NOCTURNE

('A Midsummer Night's Dream' Op.61) Mendelssohn

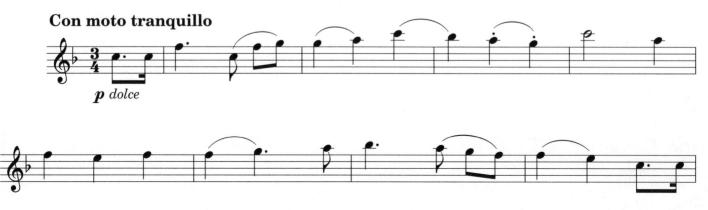

NON PIÙ ANDRAI

('The Marriage of Figaro') Mozart

O FOR THE WINGS OF A DOVE

('Hear My Prayer') Mendelssohn

ODE TO JOY

(Symphony No.9 Op.125, 4th movement) Beethoven

ONE FINE DAY

('Madame Butterfly') Puccini

PAVANE

(Op.50) Fauré

Allegro moderato

PIANO CONCERTO

(Op.16, 1st movement) Grieg

Allegro molto moderato ♩=84

PIANO CONCERTO – 'ELVIRA MADIGAN'

(K.467, 2nd movement) Mozart

PIANO CONCERTO NO.1

(Op.23, 1st movement) Tchaikovsky

PIANO CONCERTO NO.3

(Op.37, 1st movement) Beethoven

Allegro con brio

PIANO CONCERTO NO.5 – 'THE EMPEROR'

(Op.73, 2nd movement) Beethoven

Adagio un poco mosso

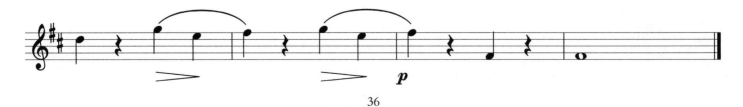

POLOVTSIAN DANCES

('Prince Igor') Borodin

PIE JESU

(Requiem Op.48) Fauré

POMP & CIRCUMSTANCE MARCH NO.4

(Op.39) Elgar

POOR WAND'RING ONE

('The Pirates Of Penzance') Sullivan

PRELUDE

(L'Arlésienne Suite No.1) Bizet

PRELUDE TO ACT III

('Lohengrin') Wagner

PROMENADE

(Pictures At An Exhibition) Mussorgsky

Allegro giusto, nel modo russico; senza allegrezza, ma poco sostenuto

PRINCE IGOR OVERTURE

Borodin

RADETSKY MARCH

(Op.228) Strauss

ROMEO AND JULIET

(Fantasy Overture) Tchaikovsky

Allegro giusto

RONDEAU

('Abdelazar') Purcell

ROSAMUNDE

(Entr'acte Act III) Schubert

SALUT D'AMOUR

(Op.12) Elgar

Andantino

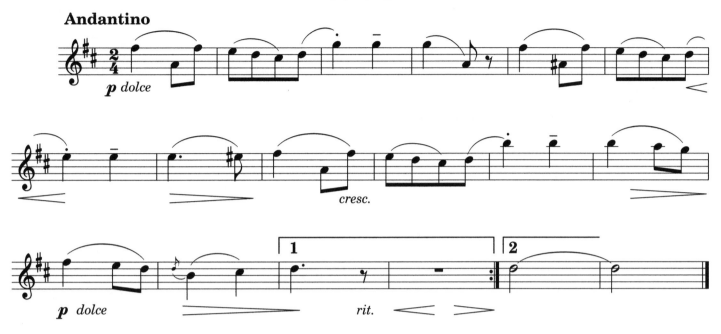

SERENADE

Schubert

Moderato

SPARTACUS – 'THE ONEDIN LINE'

Khatchaturian

SPRING

(The Four Seasons, No.1, 1st movement) Vivaldi

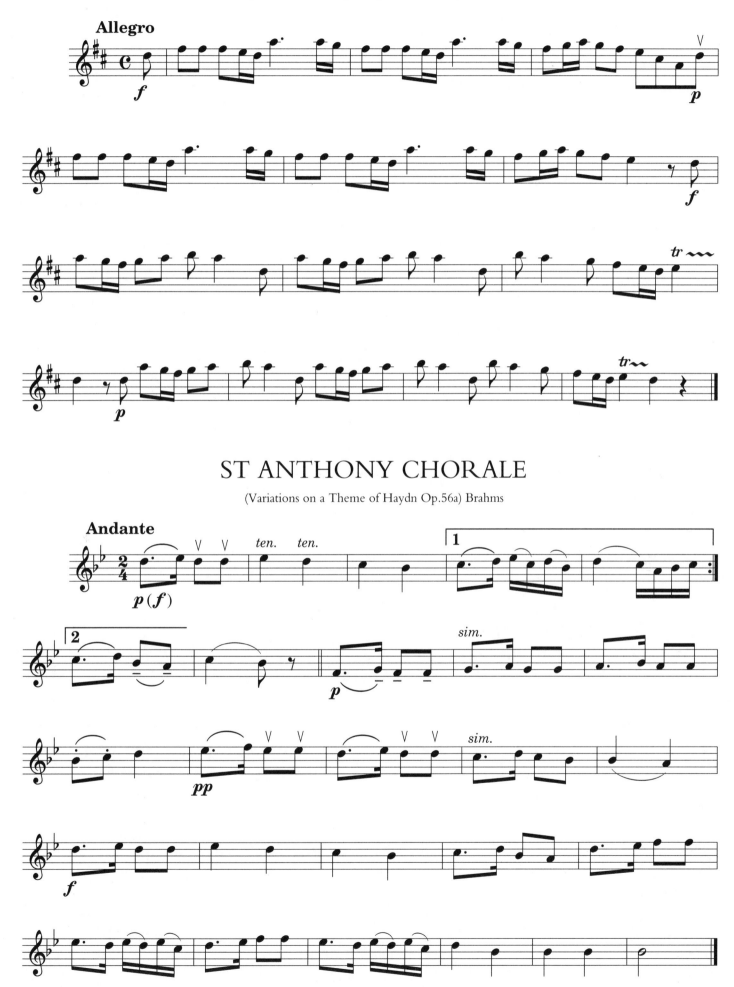

ST ANTHONY CHORALE

(Variations on a Theme of Haydn Op.56a) Brahms

SWAN LAKE

(Op.20, Opening of Act II) Tchaikovsky

SYMPHONIE FANTASTIQUE

(Op.14, 4th movement) Berlioz

SYMPHONY NO.1

(Op.68, 4th movement) Brahms

Allegro non troppo ma con brio

SYMPHONY NO.3

(Op.90, 3rd movement) Brahms

Poco allegretto

SYMPHONY NO.3 – 'THE EROICA'

(Op.55, 2nd movement)

SYMPHONY NO.5

(Op.64, 2nd movement) Tchaikovsky

SYMPHONY NO.6 – 'THE PASTORAL'

(Op.68, 5th movement) Beethoven

SYMPHONY NO.6 – 'THE PATHÉTIQUE'

(Op.74, 1st movement) Tchaikovsky

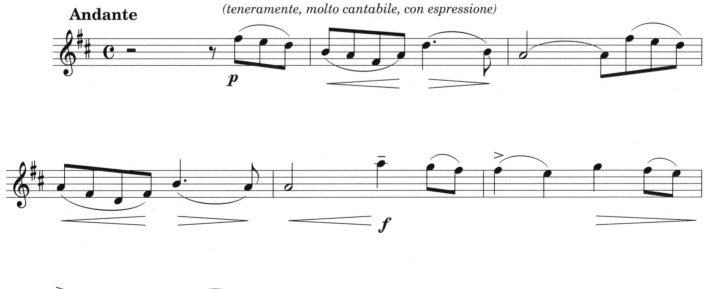

SYMPHONY NO.9 – 'THE GREAT'

(2nd movement) Schubert

SYMPHONY NO.9 – 'NEW WORLD'

(Op.95, 2nd movement) Dvořák

SYMPHONY NO.9 – 'NEW WORLD'

(Op.95, 4th movement) Dvořák

SYMPHONY NO.94 – 'THE SURPRISE'

(2nd movement) Haydn

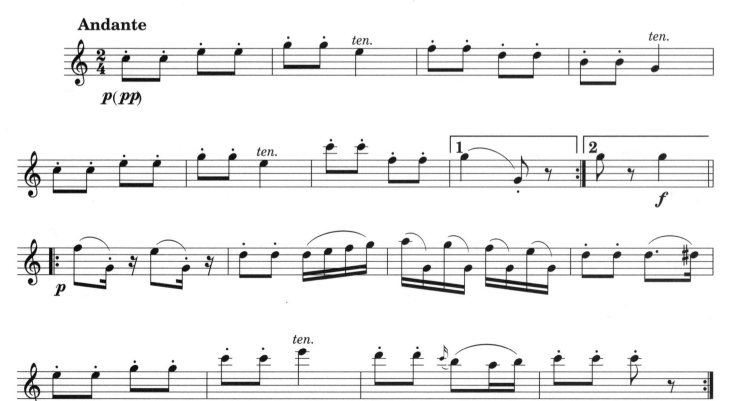

TAKE A PAIR OF SPARKLING EYES

('The Gondoliers') Sullivan

Allegretto moderato

TANNHÄUSER OVERTURE

Wagner

Andante maestoso

THE BLUE DANUBE

(Waltz, Op.314) Strauss

Tempo di valse

THE MERRY PEASANT

(Album for the Young Op.68 No.10) Schumann

THE TROUT PIANO QUINTET

(4th movement) Schubert

TORREADOR'S SONG

('Carmen') Bizet

[Alla marcia]

TRISTESSE

(Étude Op.10 No.3) Chopin

Lento, ma non troppo

TRUMPET VOLUNTARY

('The Prince of Denmark's March') Clarke

VALSE

('Coppélia') Delibes

VIOLIN CONCERTO

(Op.77, 2nd movement) Brahms

VIOLIN CONCERTO

(Op.61, 2nd movement) Elgar

VIOLIN CONCERTO

(Op.64, 2nd movement) Mendelssohn

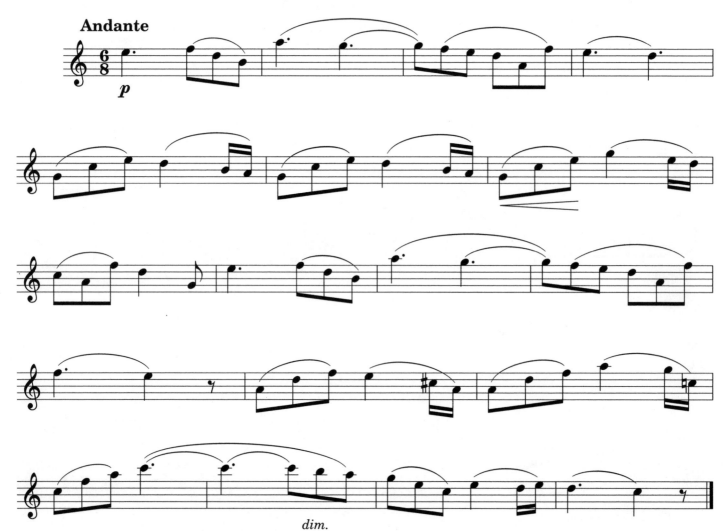

WALTZ

('The Sleeping Beauty' Op.66) Tchaikovsky

Allegro (tempo di valse)

p cantabile

più f

f

cresc.

f

WEDDING MARCH

('A Midsummer Night's Dream' Op.61) Mendelssohn

WILLIAM TELL OVERTURE

Rossini

YOUR TINY HAND IS FROZEN

('La Bohème') Puccini

24th CAPRICE FOR SOLO VIOLIN

Paganini